LEARN
SPLUNK
IN
24 HOURS
FOR
BEGINNERS

A beginner's guide to Splunk
Software

Disclaimer:

The information and materials presented here are for educational purposes only. Every effort has been made to make this book as complete and as accurate as possible but no warranty or fitness is implied. The information provided is on an "as is" basis. The ideas and opinions expressed are of the author's own imagination and the author is not affiliated to any organization, school or educational discipline and will not be held accountable or liable for any inadvertent misrepresentation.

Contents

Chapter 1: Splunk Introduction

1.1 : What is Splunk?

- Splunk is a software which is used to analyze big machine data which comes from any application. It reads and processes the unstructured, semi-structured or rarely structured big data.

- Splunk takes the big data and breaks it into individual **events** and stores it in **indexes** to enable the user to search, tag, create reports and visualization dashboards on those big data.

- Splunk has three main components:

    o **Splunk Forwarder** – It is used to gather the data and forward the data to Splunk Indexer.

    o **Splunk Indexer** – It is used for parsing and indexing the data.

    o **Search Head** – It is a graphical user interface used for searching, analyzing and reporting.

1.2 : What is Splunk Enterprise?

Splunk Enterprise is a software product that takes in data from applications and enables the user to search, analyze, and visualize the data gathered from the component.

1.3 : Download and Installation of Splunk Enterprise

➤ Google and search for *download splunk enterprise* as shown in the screen shot below.

download splunk enterprise

Q All   ▶ Videos   🖼 News   🖾 Images   ⊘ Shopping   ⋮ More

About 828,000 results (0.43 seconds)

Ad · https://www.splunk.com/enterprise   ⋮

Download Now - Splunk Enterprise

Search, analyze, and visualize your data with powerful, visually-compelling dashboa **Splunk Enterprise** free for 60 days. No credit card required. Simplify & Modernize IT.

➤ Then log into your newly created Splunk account and click on the **Download Now** button as shown in the screen shot below.

Choose Your Installation Package

| Windows | Linux | Mac OS |

| 32-bit | Windows 8.1 and 10 | .msi | Download Now ↓ |
| 64-bit | Windows 10
Windows Server 2012, 2012 R2, 2016, 2019 | .msi | Download Now ↓ |

Release Notes | System Requirements | Older Releases | All Other Downloads

Getting Data In   Sea

splunk-8.2.6-a6fe1....msi
317/375 MB, 14 secs left

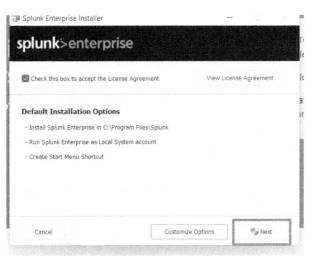

Splunk Enterprise Installer

splunk>enterprise

☑ Check this box to accept the License Agreement   View License Agreement

Default Installation Options

- Install Splunk Enterprise in C:\Program Files\Splunk
- Run Splunk Enterprise as Local System account
- Create Start Menu Shortcut

Cancel   Customize Options   Next

> Enter your desired username and password and click **Next**.

> Click on the Finish button and log into your local Splunk account using the credentials you set up while installing Splunk Enterprise.

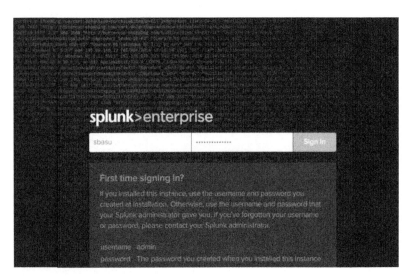

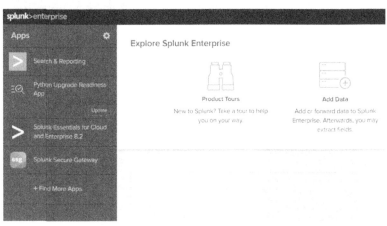

Chapter 2: Splunk Commands

2.1 : Add data in Splunk Enterprise

➢ Open an excel file and create a basic *employee* table.

employee_joining_date_timestamp	employee_id	employee_name	employee_address	employee_department	employee_salary
4/4/2020	123 Sid	Texas	admin	40000
8/8/2020	345 Kim	California	Tester	40000
12/15/2020	567 Ram	New York	Developer	50000
3/3/2021	789 John	Texas	Developer	50000
6/6/2021	910 Ron	California	admin	40000
9/9/2021	112 Jack	New York	Tester	40000
1/6/2022	121 Rim	Texas	Developer	50000

➢ Save the file as csv file.

employee
Excel Workbook (*.xlsx)
Excel Workbook (*.xlsx)
Excel Macro-Enabled Workbook (*.xlsm)
Excel Binary Workbook (*.xlsb)
Excel 97-2003 Workbook (*.xls)
CSV UTF-8 (Comma delimited) (*.csv)
XML Data (*.xml)
Single File Web Page (*.mht, *.mhtml)
Web Page (*.htm, *.html)
Excel Template (*.xltx)
Excel Macro-Enabled Template (*.xltm)

➢ Open your Splunk Enterprise -> go to **Settings** -> from there **Add Data** as shown in the screen shot below.

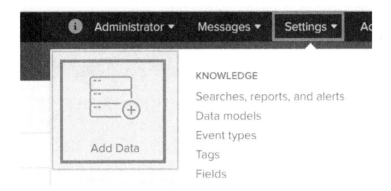

➢ Upload the newly created csv file as shown in the screen shots below.

Click on **Upload files from my computer** -> **Select File** and upload the newly created csv file -> **Next** -> **Next** -> **Review**.

Or get data in with the following methods

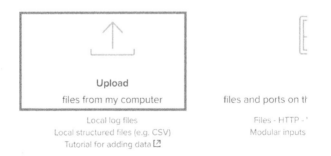

Select Source

Choose a file to upload to the Splunk platform, either by browsi

Selected File: **employee.csv**

Select File

		_time	employee_address ⬍	employee_department ⬍	employee_id ⬍	employee_joinin
1	⚠	6/4/22 5:12:24.000 PM	Texas	admin	123	4/4/2020
2	⚠	6/4/22 5:12:24.000 PM	California	Tester	345	8/8/2020
3	⚠	6/4/22 5:12:24.000 PM	New York	Developer	567	12/15/2020
4	⚠	6/4/22 5:12:24.000 PM	Texas	Developer	789	3/3/2021
5	⚠	6/4/22 5:12:24.000 PM	California	admin	910	6/6/2021
6	⚠	6/4/22 5:12:24.000 PM	New York	Tester	112	9/9/2021

Now let's start working with some of the most important and commonly used Splunk commands.

2.2 : Splunk Index

Splunk Enterprise transforms incoming data into **events,** which it stores in **indexes**.

Let's search for all the newly created index.

Open Splunk Enterprise -> Click on **Search & Reporting**

In the search bar write **index** = * -> select the time range -> press enter or click on the search icon as shown in the screen shot below. All records from the newly imported csv file should show up.

> **NOTE:** To search across all public indexes, **index** = * command is used.

i	Time	Event
>	6/8/22 9:13:21.000 AM	7/6/2022,167,Din,Virginia,Developer,60000
		host = sbasu-new source = employee.csv sourcetype = csv
>	6/8/22 9:13:21.000 AM	5/6/2022,156,Him,Virginia,CEO,100000
		host = sbasu-new source = employee.csv sourcetype = csv
>	6/8/22 9:13:21.000 AM	4/4/2022,151,Fin,Texas,Tester,40000
		host = sbasu-new source = employee.csv sourcetype = csv
>	6/8/22 9:13:21.000 AM	3/3/2022,141,Tim,New York,Developer,60000
		host = sbasu-new source = employee.csv sourcetype = csv
>	6/4/22 5:15:17.000 PM	1/6/2022,121,Rim,Texas,Developer,50000
		host = sbasu-new source = employee.csv sourcetype = csv
>	6/4/22 5:15:17.000 PM	9/9/2021,112,Jack,New York,Tester,40000
		host = sbasu-new source = employee.csv sourcetype = csv
>	6/4/22 5:15:17.000 PM	6/6/2021,910,Ron,California ,admin,40000
		host = sbasu-new source = employee.csv sourcetype = csv
>	6/4/22 5:15:17.000 PM	3/3/2021,789,John,Texas,Developer,50000
		host = sbasu-new source = employee.csv sourcetype = csv

Now we only want to display records from our newly imported csv file (*imported in section 2.1*).
Click on **source** -> select the name of your file as shown in the screen shot below.

New Search

index = * source="employee.csv"

✓ **7 events** (6/3/22 5:00:00.000 PM to 6/4/22 5:17:14.000 PM)   Nc

Events (7)   Patterns   Statistics   Visualization

Format Timeline ▾   — Zoom Out   + Zoom to Selection

6/8/22 9:13:21.000 AM	7/6/2022,167,Din,Virginia,Developer,60000
	host = sbasu-new source = employee.csv sourcetype = csv
6/8/22 9:13:21.000 AM	5/6/2022,156,Him,Virginia,CEO,100000
	host = sbasu-new source = employee.csv sourcetype = csv
6/8/22 9:13:21.000 AM	4/4/2022,151,Fin,Texas,Tester,40000
	host = sbasu-new source = employee.csv sourcetype = csv
6/8/22 9:13:21.000 AM	3/3/2022,141,Tim,New York,Developer,60000
	host = sbasu-new source = employee.csv sourcetype = csv
6/4/22 5:15:17.000 PM	1/6/2022,121,Rim,Texas,Developer,50000
	host = sbasu-new source = employee.csv sourcetype = csv
6/4/22 5:15:17.000 PM	9/9/2021,112,Jack,New York,Tester,40000
	host = sbasu-new source = employee.csv sourcetype = csv
6/4/22 5:15:17.000 PM	6/6/2021,910,Ron,California ,admin,40000
	host = sbasu-new source = employee.csv sourcetype = csv

In the above section we queried and generated records from our newly imported csv file (*employee.csv*) which was added in section 2.1.

Now click on the drop-down button highlighted in the screen shot below and select the time range within which you would like your query to be executed.

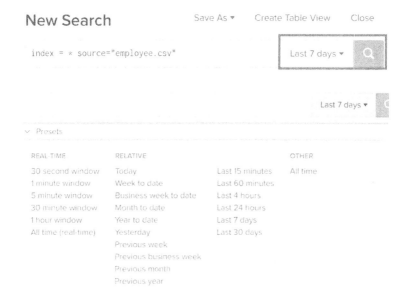

Once you select your desired time range and hit enter, your results for that time range will generate.

Comparison Operator	Description
==	Equals : x == y
!=	Not Equal x != y
<	Less than x < y
>	Greater than x > y
<=	Less than or equal to x <= y
>=	Greater than or equal to x >= y

Boolean Operator	Description
AND	Example: if x == "John" and y == "123", execute certain block of code if both statements are TRUE
OR	Example: if x == "Sid" or y == "Kim", execute certain block of code if one of the statements is TRUE
NOT	Example: score NOT (90 OR 80), execute certain block of code where score is not 90 or 80.

2.5 : Stats Command

Stats command is used to calculate aggregate functions like count, average, sum.

Syntax:-
stats *function_name*
or
stats *function_name* (*column_name or field_name*)

or

stats *function_name* **by** *column_name or field_name*

by clause is used for grouping records by specified column or field name.

Example 1

New Search

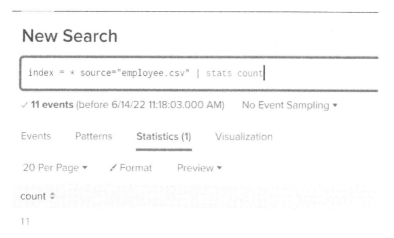

```
index = * source="employee.csv" | stats count
```

✓ **11 events** (before 6/14/22 11:18:03.000 AM)   No Event Sampling ▾

Events   Patterns   **Statistics (1)**   Visualization

20 Per Page ▾   ✐ Format   Preview ▾

count ⬍

11

The above query gets the total count of all the records present in *employee.csv* file.

NOTE: In Splunk, a vertical bar or pipe (|) is used to chain together different commands.

Example 2

New Search

```
index = * source="employee.csv" | stats count("employee_id")
```

✓ **11 events** (before 6/14/22 11:35:23.000 AM)   No Event Sampling ▾

Events   Patterns   **Statistics (1)**   Visualization

20 Per Page ▾   ∕ Format   Preview ▾

count(employee_id) ⇕

11

The above query gets the total count of *employee_id* present in *employee.csv* file.

Example 3

New Search

```
index = * source="employee.csv" | stats count(employee_id) by employee_address
```

✓ **11 events** (before 6/14/22 11:38:51.000 AM)   No Event Sampling ▾

employee_address ⇕	count(employee_id) ⇕ ✏
California	2
New York	3
Texas	4
Virginia	2

The above piece of query gets the total count of employees by *employee_address* or state. Let me simplify the concept.. the above query takes all the distinct values specified by the **by** clause. Then it gets the record belonging to that distinct value, groups them and shows the total count. In *California*, 2 employees are present, in *New York* 3 employees are present and so on.

Example 4

New Search

```
index = * source="employee.csv" | stats sum(employee_salary) by employee_address
```

✓ **11 events** (before 6/14/22 11:50:21.000 AM)   No Event Sampling ▾

employee_address ⇕	sum(employee_salary) ⇕ ✏
California	80000
New York	150000
Texas	180000
Virginia	160000

The above piece of query sums and calculates the total salary by *employee_address* or state.

Example 5

New Search

```
index = * source="employee.csv" | stats avg(employee_salary) by employee_address
```

employee_address ⬍	avg(employee_salary) ⬍ ✏
California	40000
New York	50000
Texas	45000
Virginia	80000

The above piece of query calculates the average salary by *employee_address* or state.

Example 6

Search   Analytics   Datasets   Reports   Alerts   Dashboards

New Search

```
index = * source="employee.csv" | stats max(employee_salary) by employee_address
```

employee_address ⇕	max(employee_salary) ⇕ ✎
California	40000
New York	60000
Texas	50000
Virginia	100000

The above piece of query shows the max employee salary amount each distinct *employee_address* or state holds.

Example 7

New Search

```
index = * source="employee.csv" | stats min(employee_salary) by employee_address
```

✓ **11 events** (before 6/15/22 3:57:50.000 PM)   No Event Sampling ▾

employee_address ⇕	min(employee_salary) ⇕ ✎
California	40000
New York	40000
Texas	40000
Virginia	60000

The above piece of query shows the min employee salary amount each distinct *employee_address* or state holds.

2.6 : Rename Command

Rename command helps to rename a field.

Syntax :
| **rename** *field_name* **as** *desired_name*

Example 1

New Search

```
index = * source="employee.csv" | stats count(employee_id) by employee_address | rename count(employee_id) as total_employee
```

✓ **11 events** (before 6/15/22 4:04:50.000 PM)   No Event Sampling ▾

employee_address ⇕	total_employee ⇕ 🖉
California	2
New York	3
Texas	4
Virginia	2

Example 2

NOTE: You can also rename a field by using **as** keyword instead of using the whole **rename** command

New Search

```
index = * source="employee.csv" | stats count(employee_id) as total_employee by employee_address
```

√ **11 events** (before 6/15/22 4:13.04.000 PM)   No Event Sampling ▾

employee_address ⇕	total_employee ⇕ ✎
California	2
New York	3
Texas	4
Virginia	2

2.7 : Top Command

Top command is used to find the most common values in a field. It also gives information like the count and the percentage of the frequency.

New Search

```
index = * source="employee.csv" | top limit=1 employee_salary
```

employee_salary ⇕ ✎	count ⇕ ✎	percent ⇕
40000	4	57.142852

> **Note:** limit keyword is used to limit the number of records.

25

Sort command sorts the result in ascending order or descending order.

Example 1

New Search

```
index = * source="employee.csv" | sort employee_name
```

✓ **7 events** (5/30/22 10:00:00.000 AM to 6/6/22 10:39:21.000 AM

Time	Event
6/4/22 5:15:17.000 PM	9/9/2021,112,Jack,New York,Tester,40000
	host = sbasu-new source = employee.csv sourcetype = csv
6/4/22 5:15:17.000 PM	3/3/2021,789,John,Texas,Developer,50000
	host = sbasu-new source = employee.csv sourcetype = csv
6/4/22 5:15:17.000 PM	8/8/2020,345,Kim,California ,Tester,40000
	host = sbasu-new source = employee.csv sourcetype = csv
6/4/22 5:15:17.000 PM	12/15/2020,567,Ram,New York,Developer,50000
	host = sbasu-new source = employee.csv sourcetype = csv
6/4/22 5:15:17.000 PM	1/6/2022,121,Rim,Texas,Developer,50000
	host = sbasu-new source = employee.csv sourcetype = csv
6/4/22 5:15:17.000 PM	6/6/2021,910,Ron,California ,admin,40000
	host = sbasu-new source = employee.csv sourcetype = csv
6/4/22 5:15:17.000 PM	4/4/2020,123,Sid,Texas,admin,40000
	host = sbasu-new source = employee.csv sourcetype = cs

Example 2

New Search

```
index = * source="employee.csv" | sort -employee_name
```

✓ **7 events** (5/30/22 10:00:00.000 AM to 6/6/22 10:43:12.000 AM

i	Time	Event
>	6/4/22 5:15:17.000 PM	4/4/2020,123,Sid,Texas,admin,40000 host = sbasu-new source = employee.csv sourcetype = csv
>	6/4/22 5:15:17.000 PM	6/6/2021,910,Ron,California ,admin,40000 host = sbasu-new source = employee.csv sourcetype = csv
>	6/4/22 5:15:17.000 PM	1/6/2022,121,Rim,Texas,Developer,50000 host = sbasu-new source = employee.csv sourcetype = csv
>	6/4/22 5:15:17.000 PM	12/15/2020,567,Ram,New York,Developer,50000 host = sbasu-new source = employee.csv sourcetype = csv
>	6/4/22 5:15:17.000 PM	8/8/2020,345,Kim,California ,Tester,40000 host = sbasu-new source = employee.csv sourcetype = csv
>	6/4/22 5:15:17.000 PM	3/3/2021,789,John,Texas,Developer,50000 host = sbasu-new source = employee.csv sourcetype = csv

2.9 : Table Command and Eval Command

- **table** command will take your search results and output the results into a tabular format.

- **eval** command is used to calculate an expression and puts the value into a destination field.

Syntax:

> Eval concatenation

eval *new_fieldname = field_name1 + " any joining word or punctuation " + field_name2*

Example 1

New Search

```
index = * source="employee.csv" | eval full_info = employee_id+ "_" +employee_name | table employee_id,employee_name,full_inf
```

index = * source = "employee.csv" | eval full_info = employee_id+ "_" +employee_name | table employee_id,employee_name,full_info

employee_id ⬍ ✓	employee_name ⬍	✓	full_info ⬍
121	Rim		121_Rim
112	Jack		112_Jack
910	Ron		910_Ron
789	John		789_John
567	Ram		567_Ram
345	Kim		345_Kim
123	Sid		123_Sid

> Eval case

eval *new_fieldname =* **case** *(condition1, if condition1 is true then print this, condition2, if condition2 is true then print this and so on)*

Example 2

index = * source="employee.csv" | eval dept_salary = case(employee_salary = 50000, 'high salary',1=1,'avg salary') | table employee_id,employee_name,dept_salary | sort employee_id

index = * source = "employee.csv" | eval dept_salary = case (employee_salary = 50000, "high salary", 1 = 1, "avg salary") | table employee_id, employee_name, dept_salary | sort employee_id

employee_id ⇕ ✓	employee_name ⇕	✓	dept_salary ⇕
112	Jack		avg salary
121	Rim		high salary
123	Sid		avg salary
345	Kim		avg salary
567	Ram		high salary
789	John		high salary
910	Ron		avg salary

> ## Eval if
> **eval** *field_name* = **if** (*condition, if condition is true print this, if condition is not true then print this*)

Example 3

index = * source="employee.csv" | eval dept_salary = if(employee_salary = 50000,'good salary','fair salary") | table employee_id,employee_name ,dept_salary | sort employee_id

index = * source = "employee.csv" | eval dept_salary = if (employee_salary = 50000, "good salary", "fair salary") | table employee_id, employee_name, dept_salary | sort employee_id

employee_id ⇕ ✎	employee_name ⇕	✎	dept_salary ⇕
112	Jack		fair salary
121	Rim		good salary
123	Sid		fair salary
345	Kim		fair salary
567	Ram		good salary
789	John		good salary
910	Ron		fair salary

2.10 : Where Command

Splunk **where** command is very much like SQL **where** command, only the syntax is different.

Example 1

```
index = * source="employee.csv" | where employee_name = "John" | table *
```

The above piece of query gets the record of employee whose name is *John* and displays the result in a tabular format using **table** command.

Example 2

The query below gets the total count of all the employees who does not live in *Virginia*.

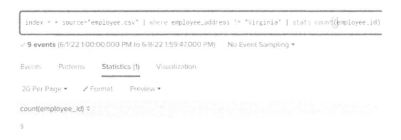

2.11 : In Command

Example 1

index = * source = "employee.csv" | where employee_address IN ("Texas" , "New York") | table employee_id, employee_department, employee_address

In the above query we are finding list of employees who live in *Texas* and *New York* and then we display the result in table format showing only the columns *employee_id*, *employee_department* and *employee_address*.

employee_id ⬦ ✎	employee_department ⬦	✎	employee_address ⬦
151	Tester		Texas
141	Developer		New York
121	Developer		Texas
112	Tester		New York
789	Developer		Texas
567	Developer		New York
123	admin		Texas

2.12 : Search Command

As the name implies search command is used to search.

Example 1

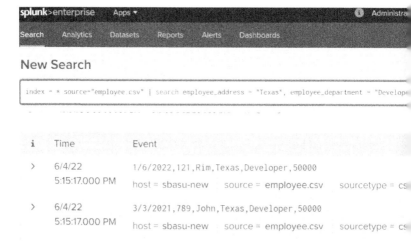

index = * source="employee.csv" | search employee_address = "Texas", employee_department = "Develope

i	Time	Event
>	6/4/22 5:15:17.000 PM	1/6/2022,121,Rim,Texas,Developer,50000 host = sbasu-new source = employee.csv sourcetype = cs
>	6/4/22 5:15:17.000 PM	3/3/2021,789,John,Texas,Developer,50000 host = sbasu-new source = employee.csv sourcetype = cs

2.13 : Wildcard

In Splunk, you can use wildcards like *, % , _ to match characters in string values. The wildcard that you use depends on the command that you are using the wildcard with:

➤ **With where command,** use the LIKE function with the percent % symbol for matching multiple characters. Use the underscore _ character to match a single character.

Example 1

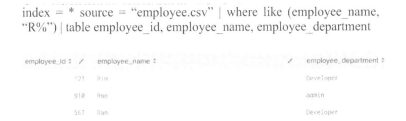

index = * source = "employee.csv" | where like (employee_name, "R%") | table employee_id, employee_name, employee_department

employee_id ⬍ ✐	employee_name ⬍	✐	employee_department ⬍
121	Rim		Developer
910	Ron		admin
567	Ram		Developer

➤ **With eval command,** use the LIKE function with the percent % symbol for matching multiple characters. Use the underscore _ character to match a single character.

Example 2

```
index = * source="employee.csv" | eval salary = if(like(employee_salary, "40%"), "decent pay", "high pay")
    | table employee_id, salary
```

index = * source = "employee.csv" | eval salary = if(like(employee_salary, "40%"), "decent pay", "high pay") | table employee_id, salary

employee_id ⇕ ✎	salary ⇕
167	high pay
156	high pay
151	decent pay
141	high pay
121	high pay
112	decent pay
910	decent pay
789	high pay
567	high pay
345	decent pay
123	decent pay

➢ With all other commands

Use the asterisk * character as a wildcard to match an unlimited number of characters in a string.

Example 3

New Search

```
index = * source="employee.csv" employee_address IN ("Vi*","Ne*")
```

✓ **5 events** (5/11/22 12:00:00.000 AM to 6/10/22 1:02:26.000 PM)   No Event

i	Time	Event
>	6/8/22 9:13:21.000 AM	7/6/2022,167,Din,Virginia,Developer,60000 host = sbasu-new source = employee.csv sourcetype = csv
>	6/8/22 9:13:21.000 AM	5/6/2022,156,Him,Virginia,CEO,100000 host = sbasu-new source = employee.csv sourcetype = csv
>	6/8/22 9:13:21.000 AM	3/3/2022,141,Tim,New York,Developer,60000 host = sbasu-new source = employee.csv sourcetype = csv
>	6/4/22 5:15:17.000 PM	9/9/2021,112,Jack,New York,Tester,40000 host = sbasu-new source = employee.csv sourcetype = csv
>	6/4/22 5:15:17.000 PM	12/15/2020,567,Ram,New York,Developer,50000 host = sbasu-new source = employee.csv sourcetype = csv

2.14 : Append Command

- Append command is used to append the result of the first query with the second query.
- The second query should be enclosed in square brackets.

Example 1

```
index = * source="employee.csv" | stats count by employee_address | append [search index = * source
    ="employee.csv" | stats avg(employee_salary) by employee_department]
```

index = * source = "employee.csv" | stats count by employee_address | append [search index = * source = "employee.csv" | stats avg(employee_salary) by employee_department]

employee_address	count	avg(employee_salary)	employee_department
California	2		
New York	3		
Texas	4		
Virginia	2		
		100000	CEO
		54000	Developer
		40000	Tester
		40000	admin

2.15 : Timechart Command

A timechart is a statistical aggregation applied to a field to produce a chart, with time used as the X-axis.

Example 1

For every 2 days calculate the number of employees added by *employee_address* or state.

New Search

```
index = * source="employee.csv" | timechart span=2d count(employee_id) by employee_address
```

index = * source = "employee.csv" | timechart span = 2d count(employee_id) by employee_address

_time ⇕	California ⇕ ✎	New York ⇕ ✎	Texas ⇕ ✎
2022-05-31	0	0	0
2022-06-02	0	0	0
2022-06-04	2	2	3
2022-06-06	0	0	0

Example 2

For every 24 hours calculate the number of employees added.

New Search

```
index = * source="employee.csv" | timechart span=24h count(employee_id)
```

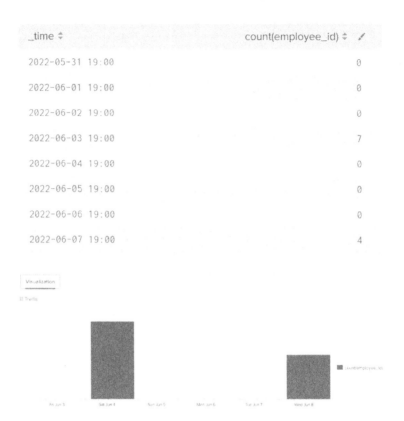

_time ⇕	count(employee_id) ⇕
2022-05-31 19:00	0
2022-06-01 19:00	0
2022-06-02 19:00	0
2022-06-03 19:00	7
2022-06-04 19:00	0
2022-06-05 19:00	0
2022-06-06 19:00	0
2022-06-07 19:00	4

2.16 : Join Command

Splunk Join command is very much like the SQL join command.

- This command returns the matching records present in two or more tables or datasets.

- The join between the two tables or dataset is performed on a common and the most important field which is present in both tables or dataset.

Syntax:
join *field_name* [*subsearch*]

Example 1

Let's create two csv files (*I created two files file1.csv and file3.csv*) and upload it in our Splunk Enterprise.

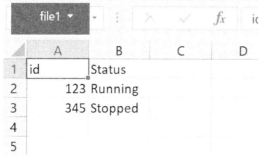

file1.csv has two fields *id* and *Status* as shown in the screen shot above.

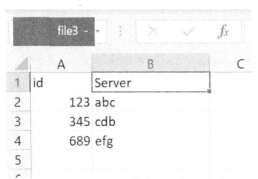

file3.csv have two fields *id* and *Server* as shown in the screen shot above.

Please Note, both the files have a common and a very important field *id* which holds data present in both the tables.

Now using Splunk, lets join the two table and generate only the matching records.

index = * source="file1.csv" | table id, Status | join id [search index = * source="file3.csv" | table id, Server]

✓ **2 events** (6/29/22 2:00:00.000 PM to 6/30/22 2:00:01.000 PM)   No Event Sampling ▾

index = * source="file1.csv" | table id, Status | join id [search index = * source="file3.csv" | table id, Server]

Let's break down the above query.

search 1 ⬇

```
index = * source="file1.csv" | table id, Status
```

common field name
present in both the tables   sub search

⬇   ⬇

```
| join id [search index = * source="file3.csv" | table id, Server]
```

id ⇕ ✎	Status ⇕	✎	Server ⇕
123	Running		abc
345	Stopped		cdb

So, we see the above query combines the two tables and prints only the matching records.

2.17 : How to create a dashboard panel

Let's write a simple query

New Search

index = * source="employee.csv" | stats count(employee_id) as total_employee, avg(employee_salary) as avg_salary by employee_address

index = * source = "employee.csv" | stats count(employee_id) as total_employee, avg(employee_salary) as avg_salary by employee_address

The query above will get the count and average salary by *employee_address* or state.

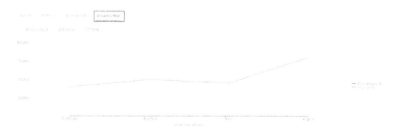

Click on **visualization** and for format I selected line chart. Now let's save it.
Click on **Save As** -> **New Dashboard**.

Give the dashboard title name -> select how do you want to build your dashboard (*I selected dashboard studio*) -> select layout mode and save.

Save Panel to New Dashboard   ✕

Dashboard Title   Employee count and average salary by state

employee_count_and_average_salary_by_state   ✎ Edit ID

Description   Optional

Permissions   🔒 Private   ▾

How do you want to build your dashboard?   What's this?

Classic Dashboards   **Dashboard Studio**   NEW
The traditional Splunk   A new builder to create visually-
dashboard builder   rich, customizable dashboards

Select layout mode

Absolute   **Grid**
Full layout control   Quick organization

                            Cancel   Save to Dashboard

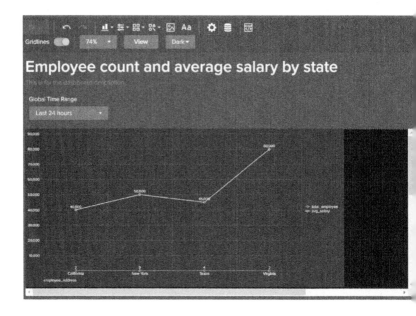

Now let's go and find the newly created dashboard.

2.18 : How to view a dashboard

➢ From Home page click on **Search & Reporting**

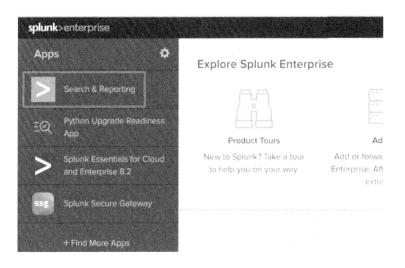

> ➤ Click on **Dashboards**

Our newly created dashboard shows highlighted in the screen shot below.

Dashboards

Dashboards include searches, visualizations, and input controls that capture and present av

Latest Resources

☆ Examples for Dashboard Studio
Browse examples of dashboards & visualizations. Visit Example Hub ↗

▥ Intro to Dashboard Studio
Learn how to build dashboards with Dashboard Studio. Learn More ↗

5 Dashboards   All   Yours   This App's

i	Title ⌃
>	Employee count and average salary by state
>	Integrity Check of Installed Files

2.19 : Creating Alerts

Let's write a query
New Search

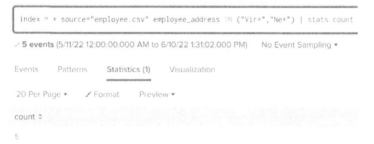

```
index = * source="employee.csv" employee_address IN ("Vir*","Ne*") | stats count
```

✓ **5 events** (5/11/22 12:00:00.000 AM to 6/10/22 1:31:02.000 PM)   No Event Sampling ▾

Events   Patterns   **Statistics (1)**   Visualization

20 Per Page ▾   ✎ Format   Preview ▾

count ⬍

5

➢ On the top right side click on **Save As** and click on **Alert**.

> Fill all the fields and click **Save**.

| Alert type | | Scheduled | | Real-time |

Run every week ▼

On   Monday ▼   at   10:00 ▼

Send log event to Splunk receiver endpoint

🔲 Output results to lookup
Output the results of the search to a CSV lookup file

Trigg

📊 Output results to telemetry endpoint
Custom action to output results to telemetry endpoint

Trig

📋 Run a script
Invoke a custom script

✉ Send email
Send an email notification to specified recipients

＞ Send to Splunk Mobile
Send a notification to Splunk Mobile recipients

+ Add Actions ▼

hour(s) ▼

umber of Results ▼

0

For each result

Cancel   **Save**

Alert has been saved ✕

⚠ This scheduled search will not run after the Splunk Enterprise Trial License expires.

You can view your alert, change additional settings, or continue editing it.

Additional Settings:

- Permissions

Continue Editing   **View Alert**

East coast employee count

Enabled: .... Yes. Disable
App: .... search
Permissions: .... Private. Owned by sbasu2302. Edit
Modified: .... Jun 10, 2022 1:44:21 PM
Alert Type: .... Scheduled. Weekly, Monday at 10:00. Edit

Trigger Condition: ... Number of Results is > 0. Edit
Actions: .... ∨ 1 Action   Edit
                              ✉ Send email

*Thank you very much for buying this book
and wish you all the best..*

Printed in Great Britain
by Amazon